DOGS
and the
People They
Own

DOGS
and the People They Own

Ed Strnad
writing as
Lillian Lidofsky

Developed by The Philip Lief Group, Inc.

A Perigee Book

A Perigee Book
Published by The Berkley Publishing Group
200 Madison Avenue
New York, NY 10016

Copyright © 1995 by The Philip Lief Group, Inc.

Book design by Joseph Perez

Cover design by James R. Harris

Cover illustration copyright © 1994 by George Booth

First edition: July 1995

Published simultaneously in Canada.

Library of Congress Cataloging-in-Publication Data

Lidofsky, Lillian.
    Dogs and the people they own / Ed Strnad writing as Lillian
Lidofsky. — 1st ed.
        p.   cm.
    "A Perigee book."
    "Developed by the Philip Lief Group, Inc."
    ISBN 0-399-51944-0
    1. Dogs—Humor.   I. Philip Lief Group.   II. Title.
PN6231.D68L53   1995
818' 25402—dc20   94-31192
                                                        CIP

Published by arrangement with The Philip Lief Group, Inc.
6 West 20th Street
New York, NY 10011

Printed in the United States of America

10   9   8   7   6   5   4   3   2   1

This book is printed on acid-free paper.

Acknowledgments

The author currishly acknowledges Denise Robert, Gary Sunshine, George Zarr, and the laptop/lapdog owners on Prodigy.

Introduction

I must tell you, after writing my first book, *Cats and the People They Own,* I was up to my *tucchus* in fan mail. All these dog people were writing me, telling me how much they enjoyed my observations on the annoying qualities of cats. "You're right," they all said, "dogs are much better!"

Now, just hold your horses. I said no such thing. And I'm not about to get mixed up in one of these "dogs vs. cats" arguments. But just to be fair, I've compiled another little list. After all, I have to be objective.

Besides, dogs are such an important aspect of our culture. Just think of the classic images of the dog: man's best friend, faithfully fetching his master's slippers and lying at his feet. . . hauling sleds through the Arctic snow. . . heroically rescuing small children from avalanches and carrying them to safety. Of course, I've never actually *seen* any dogs doing this stuff in real life. Usually, they're too busy scratching themselves or barking at the ice cream truck while it's still three blocks away.

But still, dogs are so much a part of our heritage that they've even invaded our language. Consider the many phrases that come to mind when you say the word "dog." For example, "dog-tired." I don't know how this one came about, because you don't see dogs get tired much. They always seem to be ready for a nice eighteen-mile walk, preferably at 6:00 A.M., in the rain. It's actually the human on the other end of the leash that's dog-tired. That must be it. It doesn't mean "tired *like* a dog." It means "tired *from* a dog."

Then there's "dirty dog." Now, how did that come to be the expression instead of, say, "dirty cat" or "dirty sheep" or "dirty mongoose"? Must have something to do with the dog's keen ability to zero in on any freshly moistened earth within five hundred yards, break free from their restraints, and encase themselves in a fine, crispy shell that would put any pastry chef to shame.

Or "dogged determination," so named because of the admirable persistence dogs exhibit when they want to achieve a particularly important goal—be it consuming their dinner, consuming your dinner, consuming small items of clothing and accessories, or establishing a meaningful relationship with your lower leg.

Look at the verb "to hound." It means to follow closely—i.e., nose-to-butt—making one's presence known at all times. Sound familiar?

How about "puppy love"? That's a nice one. Ever wonder where that one comes from? You might think it's supposed to suggest youthful, exuberant innocence, but in point of fact, the etymological root stems from the Latin for "pathetic drooling."

I always say, you can learn a lot about the essence of a thing by examining its linguistic connotations. To which my third husband, Leo, always says, "Huh?" He's not very bright, Leo. But he's devoted, he's loyal, and he eats whatever I put in front of him. And when he's finished, he takes off of my plate. And since he retired from the insurance company, I can't get him out from under my feet.

But you know, for some crazy reason, I love him anyway. Go figure. . .

—Lillian Ledofsky

DOGS

*and the
People They
Own*

a newspaper strike just as you're trying to

train your puppy

dogs who sigh a lot

when a dog licks his groin, *then* your hand

overpampered dogs named Buffy

people who speak baby talk to their dogs

neglecting to confirm how big, ugly, or
ill-tempered your puppy's parents were

people who say "Nice doggie"

excitable miniature dogs who are not
on Prozac

dogs wearing bandannas

countries that put Fido on the menu

dogs who are dressed like their owners

the direct relationship between lousy
weather and your dog's desire for a
long walk

discovering that the more a dog costs, the
uglier she is

puppies who mistake your new Italian
loafers for steak bones

when your dog's flatulence could kill a canary

telltale dog hair on your pillow

show-dog owners who are more psychotic
than their dogs

Scottish terriers predictably wearing
tartan clothing

French poodles inevitably named Pierre
and Fifi

when Chihuahuas try to mate with
Great Danes

pedigreed dogs who cost more than
small houses

when you can't make love because your
dog is in the room

when your significant other's dog growls
softly whenever you visit

people who say "Love me, love my dog"

that dogs are happy when someone leaves
the toilet seat up

people who train their pooches to fetch
brews from the fridge

dogs who drink your beer

Alpo breath

pooper scooper laws

pooper scooper scofflaws

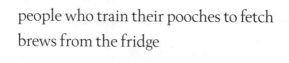

when your kid says "He followed me
home, can I keep him?"

when your dog flunks out of obedience
school

calling your mate or child by the dog's name

when your dog opens the refrigerator door
and pigs out

when Beau Geste digs a hole and lies in it
after getting a bath

having to move a seventy-pound dog
before you can get into bed

dogs that body-slam the door to be let in
instead of barking and scratching

when your dog thinks you're drowning and
tries to "rescue" you from your own pool

finding hidden dog treats in your tan pumps

chic doggy raincoats

pedigreed dogs with roman numerals
after their names

dog slobber on shined shoes

doggies who carry their own leashes

people who walk their dogs without
leashes

ostentatious rhinestone dog collars

dogs who consider a new pair of pantyhose
an invitation to jump up and say hello

when a wet dog shakes herself dry near you

150-pound dogs who still think they're little puppies

people who let their dogs lick their faces

people who let their dogs lick your face

when your dog eats chicken bones

relatives who bring their obnoxious sheepdog when they visit

when the neighbor's mutt comes through
your "pet" door and eats your dog's food

when a bitter old flame names a dog
after you

finding out firsthand why you should
never trust a calm dog

when your dog chases cars

when your dog catches cars

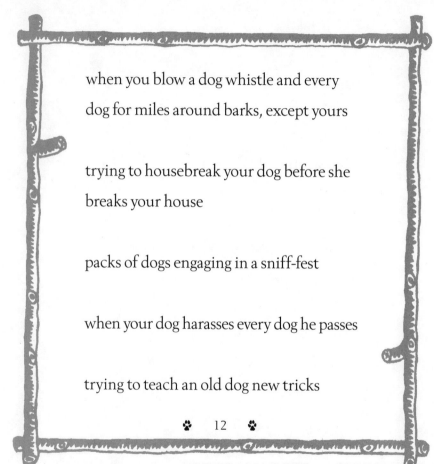

when you blow a dog whistle and every
dog for miles around barks, except yours

trying to housebreak your dog before she
breaks your house

packs of dogs engaging in a sniff-fest

when your dog harasses every dog he passes

trying to teach an old dog new tricks

❖ 12 ❖

hotels that don't allow dogs

anecdotes, folklore, and essays in praise of
animals descended from wolves

owners who talk to their dogs on the phone

when people call your pungent dog
"Old Smeller"

giving a dog a feminine name and later
discovering it's a male

owners who take offense when you call
their female dog a bitch

TV shows about dumb but lovable dogs

stubby little pugs who resemble rump
roasts on legs

suicidal strays on the freeway

when you're both master and servant to
your mutt

people who think that cats are better
than dogs

hairy little dogs that, when stretched out,
look like throw rugs

owners who find their dog's attempt to
mate with your leg quite amusing

wishing your neighbor owned a barkless
African basenji trained to curb itself

fishing with a large restless dog in a
small boat

grotesquely wrinkled shar-peis who
look like the freakish results of radiation
experiments

dogs who hallucinate and bark at
imaginary things

fuzzy stuffed puppies wearing tags saying
"I wuv you"

getting hit by frothy spit flying off an
overheated dog's tongue

when your dog *really does* eat your
homework

when your spouse blames you for the
dog's gas emission

people who don't let sleeping dogs lie

Scoobie Do's wheezy "laugh"

plucking gobs of wax out of your dog's ear

trying to get your dog to wear a seatbelt

when your dog wants to go out at
3:00 A.M.

pampered Pomeranians

dogs who will eat only premium ice cream

butt-ugly bulldogs incongruously named
"Buttercup"

people who believe that bigger is better
when it comes to dogs

dogs so big and massive that light bends
around them

small, pretty dogs owned by large,
ugly people

black dogs on white carpets

white dogs on black carpets

when your pooch has a little accident on
your satin sheets

being unable to turn in bed because of a
big dog wedged against you

that Mopsy's tail is a magnet for
precariously balanced priceless objects

when she mills around the yard
unrelieved, then performs the "squat
and fake pee" routine when scolded

when your dog barks in his sleep

when the dog steals the kid's cookies while
Junior is doing homework

the breeds that bite the most: German
shepherds, chows, and poodles

bobbing-head dog statues in car
rear windows

Millie Bush and Checkers Nixon

being set upon by a pack of wild dogs

when your big dog walks *you*

adorable puppies who become old
unwanted mutts

people who abandon their dogs

dogs who howl whenever you start to sing

the funky smell of a wet dog

little dogs who bounce up and down and
bark at the same time

people who use little dogs as baby
substitutes

dogs wearing hair ribbons

owners who pretend to be blind so they can
get Fido into a "No Dogs Allowed" hotel

the fact that nine U.S. Mail carriers are bitten by dogs each day

when your dog shakes everyone's hand but yours

dogs who like to play "catch the ball and eat it"

people who swear that their dogs can read their minds

dogs who magically appear whenever you open the refrigerator door

dinky dogs who consume their weight in
food each day

owning a spunky dog when you hate spunk

people who eat dog biscuits

dogs who resemble buffalo in size and odor

when your dog shuns the expensive
doghouse you bought her

owner-pet lookalikes, such as Winston
Churchill and his bulldog

arrogant poodles with attitude

alcoholic St. Bernards like the brandy-
lapping ghost-dog on the TV show *Topper*

having to put mouthwash in the toilet
to improve your dog's breath

dogs who piddle next to the newspaper,
rather than on it

when you inform someone that
your dog is a Shih Tzu, and they say
"Gesundheit"

when muddy, dripping Mandy dries off
on your bed

100-pound dogs who stomp all over you
until you get out of bed and feed them

when your dog opens the oven door and
licks up anything that was cooked in the
last decade

dogs who eat all the fruit off low-hanging
tree branches, then puke

that if you leave food out for your dog,
he'll eat it all immediately, not saving any
for later

when dog droppings leave brown spots on
your lawn

canines who think they're felines and
chase birds

dogs who like to roll around in
vile-smelling filth

lifting 50-pound bags of dry dog food

a dog's ability to inflict guilt whenever
you eat something in front of her

dogs with weak bladders

dogs with loose stools

dogs who must perform long complicated
rituals before excreting any bodily wastes

when your dog eats whipped cream and is
mistaken for a rabid dog

the overabundance of movies involving a
cop with a canine partner

when prodigiously endowed dogs become
aroused in front of polite company

when a barking dog in a passing car makes
you jump off the ground

people who walk two or more dogs
simultaneously

wondering why Pekingese are not now
known as "Bejingese"

❖   29   ❖

people who grin dopily while gazing upon
the latest coffee-table book about dogs

dogs who sleep under the covers

discovering the truth to the maxim
"When you lie with dogs, you're gonna
get fleas"

owning a dog who wants to kill *anyone*
who comes to the front door

when your dog chews up the letters
that come through the mail slot, but
not the bills

trying to play tennis when there's a dog on
the court

a dog whose bite *is* worse than his bark

submissive dogs who won't look you
in the eye

when big energetic pooches are kept
cooped up in tiny apartments

knowing that Pete the Dog in *The Little
Rascals* was a pit bull

people who train their pit bulls to
be vicious

owners who exaggerate their dogs'
intelligence, lovableness, etc.

people who anthropomorphize
their dogs

when people walk dogs in baby carriages

pictures of doggies wearing big sunglasses
and hats

Wegman's "Man Ray" photographs

"people biscuits" for dogs

pups wearing tailored pants

dogs who get to the gift chocolates before
you do

heartwarming dog stories on slow news days

getting busted by a police dog

❖   33   ❖

taking the dog for a walk after he's been
constipated for several days

when your dog's haircut costs more than
yours and looks better

discovering that well-fed dogs have
recently visited your golf course

dogs named Killer

owners who have hairier ears than
their dogs

the song "Me and You and a Dog
Named Boo"

doggie dandruff

having to hang a pork chop around your
neck so your dog will like you

when Spot dumps your garbage can and
rummages through it

when your sweet puppy turns into Cujo

people who own one large dog, and one
small dog, as a spare

peppy pups with high WPMs (wags
per minute)

stringy haired komondors who could do
double-duty as mops

disgustingly healthy dogs that will
probably outlive you

Benji movie marathons

high-speed tail waggers

when a dog digs up your garden burying
a bone

yellow snow

making snow angels in yellow snow

people who think dogs show remorse

crazed aggressive mastiffs

high-energy (read "hyper") basenjis

when your rottweiler consumes more
food daily than you

cutesy Maltese that look like stuffed animals

that modern dogs have been bred into
creatures that aren't quite dogs anymore

pricey dog-grooming salons

lost dogs lacking ID tags

dogs that require several long walks a day

throwing a gross, slimy, spit-soaked tennis
ball to your retriever

people who have their dogs' portraits
painted

that "Xoloitzcuintli" is actually a dog
breed, not a line from an eye chart

electric fences that shock dogs

being unable to pronounce "Lhasa Apso"
without spitting

the fact that one flea can lay more than
2,000 eggs in its lifetime

that dogs are basically mobile homes for
fleas, ticks, and vermin

dogs with crossing-the-street phobias

W.C. Fields's line "Anyone who hates kids
and dogs can't be all bad"

Keane's paintings of dogs and kids with
huge weepy eyes

being born during the Chinese Year
of the Dog

that no one can take a beagle seriously

neighbors who leave their yapping dogs
outside all day and night

lying awake listening to a neighbor's
barking dog

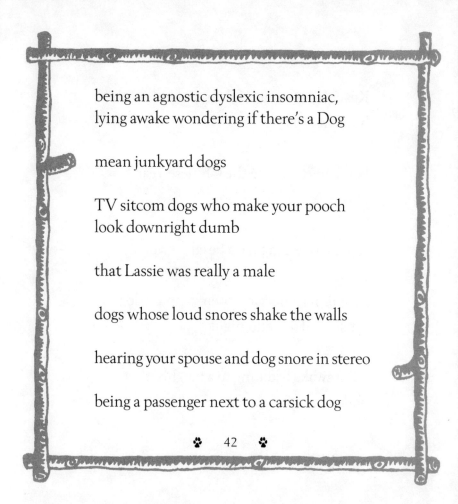

being an agnostic dyslexic insomniac,
lying awake wondering if there's a Dog

mean junkyard dogs

TV sitcom dogs who make your pooch
look downright dumb

that Lassie was really a male

dogs whose loud snores shake the walls

hearing your spouse and dog snore in stereo

being a passenger next to a carsick dog

ugly bulldogs who always have threads of
drool dangling from their jowls

lethargic dogs whose only trick is
playing dead

"Have You Hugged Your (dog breed)
Today?" bumper stickers

dogs who won't fetch

dogs who catch balls but won't give
them back

when your dog chases a cat that turns out
to be a skunk

having to bathe your skunk-sprayed dog in
tomato juice

having to put your paunchy pet on a diet

trying to decide which is more annoying,
woof-woof barks or *ruff-ruff* barks

machine-gun barks: rah-rah-rah... rah-rah-
rah... rah... rah-rah-rah... rah...

when your dog is a furry four-legged pervert

when your dog continues to lift his leg
even when his bladder's empty

a mongrel called "Heinz" because he's 57
varieties

when your sexually frustrated dog
starts looking at the family cat with lust
in his heart

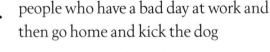

people who have a bad day at work and
then go home and kick the dog

dogs who act a little too human

having to walk head-down in the city to
avoid "land mines" on the sidewalk

owners fond of dropping doggy-phrases
into their speech, e.g., "doggone,"
"dogged," "dog-tired"

New Yorkers who say "dawg"

Californians who say "dahg"

when your lively fun-loving puppy
matures into a sedate frumpy dog

the millions of terriers who have been
named Toto

the millions of beagles who have been
named Snoopy

dogs wearing fanny packs

that the old "Underdog" balloon is still in
the Macy's Thanksgiving Day Parade,
when no kid knows who he is

when a dog catches the newspaper and tries
to bring it back to the delivery person

having to walk your dog on a sub-zero night

dogs who must sniff and pee on every tree, pole, and vertical landmark in sight

that dogs merely scratch the ground after taking a dump, rather than burying it

when a passing car breaks your defecating doggie's concentration

dogs whose eyes are always covered by hair

weeny dogs with their tails between their legs

small dogs who always walk between your
legs and trip you

when a sneaky dog sticks out his
long tongue to filch leftovers from the
dinner table

overrated watchdog capabilities

when a neighbor's dog trespasses on your
property to chase your cats

when guests are visiting and Poochy drags
out a *very* personal piece of your clothing
from the hamper

when your dog needs a hernia operation
that costs more than your first car

lies you tell your guests, like "She doesn't
bite" and "That means she likes you"

realizing that dogs lick your hand for the
salty taste, not out of affection

having to patch up your dog's
cat-scratched nose

when a burglar sabotages your first line
of defense by throwing your guard dog
a T-bone steak

putrid cans of dog food made of
mysterious "meat by-products"

horsemeat in dog food

"gourmet" dog food

when fat bloblike dogs lie on your chest
and constrict your breathing

lazy dogs that just sleep their short
lives away

people who say you act like your dog

dirty dogs who have to be chased into the bathtub

having to rescue your dog from the undertow at the beach

dry couches and wet dogs

the superstition that a dog's howl means someone will die

being superstitious and having a dog who howls frequently

unruly dogs who never become tame and
friendly with people

trying to understand why a man's best
friend would eat his shorts

that a dog will blindly worship his master,
even when his master is a serial killer

that "intelligent" dogs never figure out
how to unwind their chains when they get
wrapped around trees

worrying why dog spelled backwards is god

when your dog has a "bad fur day"

a lost-dog poster for a one-eyed dog, missing
an ear, with a leg in a cast—who answers to
the name "Lucky"

when your dog is better groomed than
you are

discovering the idiosyncrasies—like a
shoe-chewing addiction— that caused
your adopted dog to be abandoned

losing custody of your dog in a divorce

living with a cat person when you're a
dog person

dachshunds whose bellies scrape the ground

a bloodhound's pendulous lips

people who aren't as nice as their dogs

that you'll never know what your dog
really thinks about you

wondering what your dog's pet name for
you would be

❖   55   ❖

hunting dogs trained to sniff your
private parts

people who talk to passing dogs and
ignore the dog walkers

when your dog takes a whiz on your
Garfield cartoon books

dogs addicted to hole digging

yuppies walking matching pairs of puppies

breeders who cruelly and unnecessarily
amputate dogs' tails

having to toss a bucket of cold water on
fighting dogs

people who own dogs because they haven't
got the guts to bite people themselves

that dogs tend to smell "riper" with age

when your dog does his business right in
front of your dog-hating neighbor, and on
his lawn

the icky feeling you get from petting a
Mexican hairless

the inverse relationship between the size
of a dog and its nervousness

dogs who never barf their Mighty Dog
outdoors, only indoors

the period between observing your dog
slinking guiltily and discovering his
infraction

trying to fend off a horny pup intent on
impregnating your leg

when your Pomeranian pees on the
Persian rug

when dogs keep sniffing the ground while
you're screaming for them to come

dogs who continue to lick their bowls
long after all detectable traces of food
have been eaten

car windows smeared with dog snot

dogs strong enough to pull a tractor with
their leashes

that they don't always land on their feet
like cats

dogs who chase your bike and snap at
your ankles

when your dog's taste runs toward
rotten stuff

when your dog swallows a piece of jewelry
and you have to watch for it to come out

people who send postcards to their dogs

canine cosmetic surgery to remove
unsightly hair

people who freeze-dry their deceased
dogs' corpses

wondering what Goofy the dog is doing
owning Pluto, another dog

when dogs spin around a dozen times
before they lie down

when you yell "Hey, Duke" at the park and
ten dogs turn around

fighting back tears while reading a eulogy
to a dead dog

Little Nipper's eternal befuddlement at
hearing his master's voice electronically
reproduced

dogs addicted to chasing Frisbees

doggy novelty songs, like "I'm Looking
Over My Dead Dog, Rover"

learning that "woofers" pertain to hi-fi,
and are *not* a breed of dog

dogs who tilt their heads and whimper
when they hear a harmonica

having to take a hound to the pound

when a drug-sniffing dog singles out your
suitcase at an airport

owners for whom little dogs are basically
living dolls

city dogs who snap and jump off balconies
of high-rise condos

taste-tempting doggie treats, like
Honey-Roasted Gristle Sticks,
Kitty-Shaped Gobble Bits, and
Horse-Sinew Chew Chunks

dogs with stinky leg pits

breeds that appear to be half dog, half pig

pups with bellies the color of Pepto-Bismol

that dogs are high-maintenance pets

when an unfriendly pooch curls his upper
lip and snarls at you

worming your dog

scrappy breeds that you often have to separate with sticks

cooking a can of dog food that you mistook for chili

always having a layer of dog hair on the bottom of your socks

dogs who drink out of your aquarium

when a scratching dog makes waves on your waterbed

when Rex eats your Silly Putty

people who carry dogs in the backs of
their pickup trucks

finding multicolored poop in the scooper
because someone left the crayons out

people who leave their poor, hot dogs
locked in cars

when your dog reacts to a doorbell that is
ringing on TV

purebred breeds that come with special "built-in" health problems, such as ear problems in cockers, breathing in pugs, skin in shar-peis

owners who let their dogs decide when and how much to eat

cockers who bite the leg of your jeans when you're trying to get dressed

shoe thieves who like to strew your loafers all over your house

dogs who lick the tip of your nose when
they want to go out

being given a pathetic look by a basset hound

when your dog goes on a panty raid and
hides your undies under the bed

when your pup pulls all the underwear off
the clothesline, making it look like you
had a backyard orgy

a dog whose nose is always dripping

the ridiculous positions that dogs can get
into when they mate

reading stories about loopy, big-hearted
mutts who always die at the end

wondering why calling someone "a dog" is
a term of contempt

when a dog who seems to be paying
rapt attention to your words is actually
thinking "Let's eat, you two-legged
mutant"

prissy show dogs who have never eaten
wild game

people who call dogs "almost human" and
end up insulting both species

people who are patsies for puppies

giving your heart to an animal who is
guaranteed to die before you

humans trained to open a door at the
sound of a bark

two-headed dogs created in sicko
experiments by cold-war Commies

loud foot-thumping in the middle of
the night when your dog dreams that
he's running

the fact that dog food gets its own aisle in
the supermarket

alarm systems that use unconvincing
recordings of dogs barking

ancient dogs with flies buzzing around
their heads

when you mutter "that damn mutt" more
than once a day

when sheepdogs lose their flocks

scene-stealing movie dogs

eating anything that your dog refuses
to eat

when your pooch finds pats on her head
to be condescending

those "see Spot run" books when you were
learning to read

that after a thousand generations of
living with humans, dogs still don't
understand the meaning of
"Get down"

when a dog gets too old to play

metal cages called "kennels"

that dogs probably think humans are nuts

❖   73   ❖

that dogs are not loyal to other dogs, only
to people

that all owners think their breed is the best

people who express affections for their
mutts that they withhold from their
human friends and family

coffee mugs with doggy's photo

people who risk their lives to save their
dogs from burning buildings

dogs who show their appreciation by
chewing up your home

dogs who run away

having to brush your dog's teeth

people who shower with their dogs

posh pups wearing nail polish

people who take their dogs to work
with them

people who greet their dogs first when
they come home

dog-to-friend greeting cards

when it's time to take your old dog to
Dr. Kevorkian for his checkout

nasty gossipy pit-poodles

when you drive without your hefty dog and
find you get ten more miles to the gallon

when your heavily shedding dog turns all
your carpets into shag carpets

when your dog passes gas and quickly
looks around, as if to say "Where did *that*
noise come from?"

when you push against your dog's side,
and she pushes back harder

dogs who catch social diseases from using
public lampposts

three-legged tripod dogs

when you hear a suspicious noise at
night and have to wake your dog and
make her bark

gorgeous dogs who know they are

female cocker spaniels unimaginatively
named Lady

panhandlers' dogs who do all the begging

when several dogs live under your front porch

when the major food groups of your dog's diet are beef jerky and Spam

dogs who pilfer potato chips when you're not looking

that curiosity never killed a dog

sensitive dogs who get upset when they hear family arguments

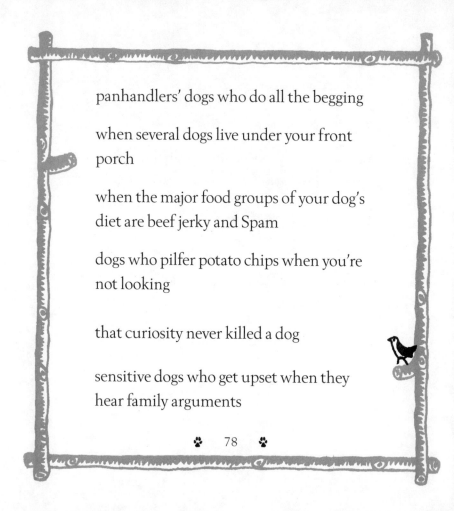

when your pooch gets purloined

kids who grew up without a dog

when your younger brother or sister got
the dog you always begged for

the musky scent on your hand after
petting a grimy dog

finding your pooch's claw-clippings in bed

people who never name their pet, just
calling it "Dog"

formerly clean city parks that have gone to the dogs

when a dog brushes against your clean suit pants

people who make their pets perform inane stunts for dog biscuits

living next to a hard-core "dogophile" who owns multiple dogs

knowing that Hitler was the devoted owner of several dogs

operatic mutts who "sing" arias to the moon

dogs on lamb and rice diets when you
can't afford lamb for yourself

when your dog launches a frenzied attack
on the vacuum cleaner

muffling the jingle of the car keys so your
sleeping dog won't wake and realize you're
going for a ride without her

movie-dog trainers who put rubber bands
around dogs' snouts to make them look as
if they're snarling

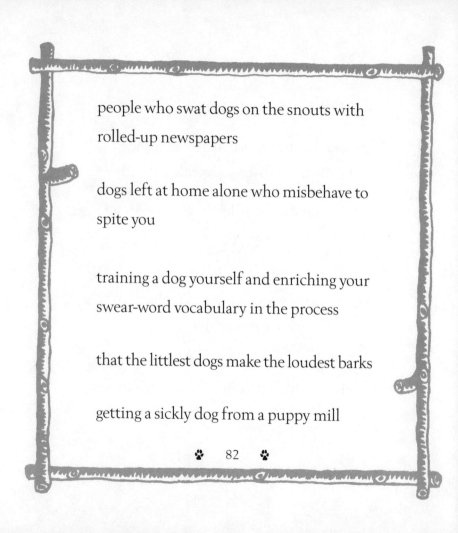

people who swat dogs on the snouts with
rolled-up newspapers

dogs left at home alone who misbehave to
spite you

training a dog yourself and enriching your
swear-word vocabulary in the process

that the littlest dogs make the loudest barks

getting a sickly dog from a puppy mill

dogs who figure out how to open pantry
doors and get into the garbage bag for a
midnight snack

doors that get scratched up from your dog
jumping on them

when your dog thinks cat turds are tasty
snacks

when the high point of your pet's day is
the opening of a tin of mystery meat

when your dog barfs in your car on the
way to the vet

when your dog sticks his head out the car
window and catches bugs in his mouth

guys who walk pairs of intimidating
macho dogs

suspecting that dogs are really super-smart
aliens feigning dependency so humans
will give them lifelong support

having to listen to a friend bragging about
how clever (loyal, devoted, etc.) his dog is

owners whose houses always have a strong
doggy smell

people who let their dogs swim in the pool
with you

people who put dogs to sleep for doing things
that come naturally, like defending turf

owning a Pekingese and hearing witty
remarks, like "Who smashed your dog's
face in with a shovel?"

dumb dogs having flat faces from chasing
parked cars

when a dog "christens" your car's tires

dogs who carry snow into the house on
their fur

the ornery bad-tempered dog owned
by the ornery bad-tempered neighbor

when your dog eats the cat's food

when Rowlf takes up all the room in your
hammock

having to board your dog in a kennel or find
a pet sitter whenever you go on vacation

owners who don't know where their dogs'
pasterns, hocks, dewlaps, croups, stifles,
or withers are

people who whistle "How Much Is That Doggy in the Window?" in pet shops

having to scoop for your dog after changing a baby's diapers all day

dogs who have fits of ecstacy when you come home, even if you've been gone only five minutes

when your neighbor's mutt impregnates your purebred dog

 people who write to you on "Snoopy" stationery

mistaking a wild wolf for a poor lost doggy

gnawed and nasty chew-toys littering
your yard

muddy paw prints tracked throughout
your house

when a dog loses his personality after
being "fixed"

that you can't deduct your dog's expenses
on your taxes

dogs who kick and thrash wildly when
you pick them up

when a Frisbee-chasing mutt runs over
you while you're tanning on the beach

large dog, small car, long trip

guys who get cute dogs just to find dates

discovering that pedigreed dogs drop like
flies, but mutts live forever

not understanding Aesop's fable about the
dog with a bone who saw his reflection

smug "I've seen it all" city dogs

when your pup chews through the
phone cord

people who have cute pictures of dogs
printed on their personal checks

wizened toothless hounds lying in the
middle of a dirt road

spending irreplaceable hours of your life
grooming a long-haired dog

clipping your dog's tough-as-nails toenails

the mean dog who barks at you every time
you walk past his house

the *click-click* sound of a dog's claws
walking on linoleum

when a dog watches your every move

when your dog goes bonkers in
anticipation of going out every time
you put on your shoes

that in most cities dogs have to be
licensed, but cats don't

dogs who wake you up for their 6:00 A.M.
walks even on weekends

blowing your cool when a dog totally
ignores your commands

when your dog doesn't consider you the
"top dog" of his pack

people who use choke collars

when the neighbor's pussycat beats up
your tough guard dog

that no dogs were allowed aboard the
Enterprise on *Star Trek*

that dogs gave their lives in the early
exploration of space

when your dog's still shedding her winter
coat in August

people who buy dogs only for warding
off muggers and burglars, not for
companionship

the insidious ability of a warm cuddly
puppy to turn a person into a dog owner

bottles of nontoxic dog shampoo that cost
more than your designer shampoos

petting a dog and having his fur come out
in clumps

the ignoble fate of old racing greyhounds

dog psychiatrists

a sneaky dog who sits on the forbidden
chair only when you're not home

when your dog learns quicker than you do

dogs who gag when they watch you eat

dogs who can flip biscuits off their noses
and catch them

circus dogs who make your dog's tricks
look crude

catalogs brimming with dog paraphernalia

flea dirt

when the temperaments of dog and owner
are mismatched

running out of bags for the scooper

owners who are sicker than sick puppies

indolent dogs who don't work like a dog

overfed dogs who resemble medium-sized
sofas

dogs who only bark at other animals,
not intruders

dogs who insist on going into the bathroom with you

people who fake throwing a ball and really
confuse their dogs

when your dog makes a mad dash out the
door the instant it opens

that the longer you own a dog, the more
irreplaceable she becomes

a neighbor's dog who whines and barks
the entire time they're away, but acts
impeccably when they're within earshot

when dogs jump up trying to catch birds
flying miles over their heads

when your dog runs headlong into a tree
chasing a squirrel

calling a mixed breed a "generic" dog

dogs having excessively clever names, like
"Howard Huge"

when your pet chews on his squeaking
vinyl pork chop in the middle of the night

when your dog gets the "seven-year itch"

acupuncture for dogs

manicures for mutts

people curiously repelled by scabby dogs

when your dog stares at you until you
feed him, walk him, or throw something
to him

when he digs an escape tunnel under
your fence

dogs who eat through wood to create their
own doggy door

dogs who have a very loose definition of
the word "edible"

the second after you smell the odor
and the second before you check the
sole of your shoe

under-the-table moochers

when a rhino-size dog steps on your foot

Huckleberry Hound's redneck drawl

people who lift dogs up by the ears

when loud bloody skirmishes break out between your dogs

mutant dogs with extra toes on each paw

when even your dog isn't glad to see you

that dogs are oblivious to their own mortality

funerals and cemeteries for dearly departed dogs

people who are embarrassed to undress in front of their dogs

musicians with canine names, such as
Three Dog Night, Bonzo Dog Band,
Snoop Doggy Dog, etc.

when your dog never warns you of
impending earthquakes

that dogs never get laryngitis after barking
for hours and hours

when your dog won't sic the people
you hate

styling gels and mousses for pooches

that any open car door is an invitation to
jump in

dogs who do everything on command,
except relieve themselves

the questionable intentions of the dog in
those Coppertone ads

when your dog's coat gets hot spots

the apocryphal story about the wet poodle
that was dried in a microwave

that any food that falls on the floor
automatically becomes the dog's property

trying to walk your dog down a steep
icy hill

paunchy pups that get liposuctioned

a mutt barking when you're trying
to think

being a dinner guest in a home where they
let the dog lick the plates clean

backseat driver dogs breathing down
your neck

drivers who don't brake for dogs

when the flea exterminator covers
your house with a Day-Glo tent the size
of Nebraska

that dog ownership means giving up the
freedom to come and go as you please

when dogs check their bowls hourly
on the off chance that some food has
magically materialized in it

owners who spend hours writing
about their pooches on computer
bulletin boards

the fact that 40,000 kids are bitten in the
face each year by their family dogs

Norman Rockwell's wrenchingly
sentimental images of sad-eyed dogs
waiting for Master

when dog saliva—which contains every
bacterium known to science—is laved onto
your cuts and scrapes

dog horoscopes

dogs who can sense your fear

psychotic dogs who attack themselves if
no one else is available

lecherous bulging bulldog eyes

when a dog giving birth gives you a termi-
nal case of "Eeyews"

the goofy looks on the faces of mating dogs

when your dog never forgives you
for getting him fixed

having to get your female dog artificially
inseminated

rabies shots

Hollywood's Dog Groomers to the Stars

dog plates, figurines, and other collectibles

trying to cure a hangover with a "hair of
the dog" and gagging instead

people who walk their dogs past the
Blarney Stone

vermin-infested doghouses

when a militant dog hangs around
outside the ASPCA shelter, barking
"Let my people go"

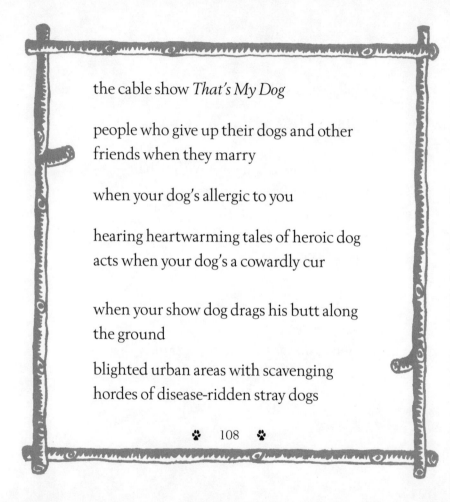

the cable show *That's My Dog*

people who give up their dogs and other
friends when they marry

when your dog's allergic to you

hearing heartwarming tales of heroic dog
acts when your dog's a cowardly cur

when your show dog drags his butt along
the ground

blighted urban areas with scavenging
hordes of disease-ridden stray dogs

walking barefoot in a befouled dog-run

that few dog barks really sound like
"bow-wow"

that dog owners live longer than those
who don't own dogs

dogs who howl at the moon even when it's
overcast

when a dog bites and punctures your
basketball

Airedales who belch on cue

pugs who appear perpetually worried

when your bone-strewn back lawn looks
like a desecrated graveyard

that a pit bull's jaws are ten times more
powerful than other dogs'

the use of "K-9" as a witty substitute for
the word "canine"

that the people on *Lassie* couldn't figure
out that the dog was always trying to tell
them Timmy was in trouble

telephones shaped like dogs

when pooch plays tug-of-war with your
pants when you're trying to get dressed

when your watchdog is the friendliest pet
in the neighborhood

slovenly dogs who need a bath every
other day

coming home dog-tired after walking your
pet for miles

dogs who wear guilty expressions all
the time

when your dog thinks your beret is a Frisbee

pups in circular pursuit of their posteriors

when your dog starts freaking out a mile away from the vet's office

wondering if you'd still own a dog if they could talk

trying to hide your dog from your apartment's no-dogs-allowed landlord

getting bitten by a "nice doggy" when you were a little kid

tail-pulling brats

people who own black and white Scottish
terriers to match their home's color scheme

people who get dogs just for the
instant peer group that dog ownership
provides

how you can say the cruelest things to
dogs, as long as you use a sweet tone
of voice

when your house looks like one big
bathroom to your pup

saying "No" a thousand times a day to
your puppy

owning a kissy-poo dog who always has
mud on her tongue

doggy bags that people eat

when your dog tries to catch a fly indoors,
wrecking your house in the process

missing those old dog-food commercials
starring Lorne Greene

older dogs who spend their days just
napping until their next meal

people who tie up their dirty dogs and
hose 'em down

when a dog tries to bite the water spraying
out of a hose

otherwise laid-back dogs who commit
mayhem when they team up

people who compare dog behavior to
human male behavior

the saying "The more I see of men, the
more I admire dogs"

when you visit a shelter and feel sorry that
you can't adopt them all

standing outside a supermarket trying to
find homes for your pet's litter

when your dog has a bigger Christmas
stocking than you

when you come home and find that
Fido made dessert out of your stereo
headphones

when your dog gets shots and saturates
the vet's lap

dogs who gnaw your favorite paperbacks,
but leave the romance novels alone

collections of ceramic dogs

when your dog scampers from room to
room as fast as he can

how every dog thumps its hind leg when
you scratch its chest

owners wearing dog-theme accessories,
such as dog T-shirts, hats, aprons, etc.

tacky tapestries of booze-swilling dogs
playing poker

people who own more dogs than the
law allows

that the rubber dog-poop gag is ineffective
on dog owners

when the only conversation you have
with your neighbor is to shout
"Get that damn mutt off my lawn"

German shepherds who walk with
goose-steps

people who bark at dogs and set the dogs
off on a barking jag

the fuss and bother involved in owning a
precious "foo-foo" dog

when your dog is always trying to get a leg
up on the local competition

the amount of news coverage lavished on
celebrity canines like Mike the Dog

Chevy Chase playing a dog detective in the
movie *Oh, Heavenly Dog*

when your dog has her litter of puppies on
the living room floor

trying to remove ticks from a frisky dog

dogs with formidable fangs

the fact that Americans annually spend
more on dog food than on charitable
contributions

clichéd pictures of a dog frozen in a midair
Frisbee catch

when your dog looks at you, takes two steps
toward the kitchen, and looks at you again

irascible dogs who bark at the slightest
provocation

when your kids lose interest in the dog
they begged you to get

❖ 120 ❖

when your pet turns into a pest

Irish setters who won't sit

dogs who frequently become airborne

dogs with big hair

when you give your significant other the
ultimatum "It's me or the dog" and you lose

when visitors unintentionally liberate
your house-restricted pets

grouchy, grumpy Great Danes

❖   121   ❖

when a dog somehow becomes a
registered voter

owners who think it's cute to make their
dogs do odd acts, like ride on a skateboard

when dogs are used in ads to sell beer, like
Spuds McKenzie

ads for bogus electronic flea collars

paying $29.95 for a puppy training video
that your puppy won't watch

repressed timid dogs who make muffled
little barks under their breath

❧ 122 ❧

being unable to identify popular "trivia dogs" such as Asta, Freeway, Astro, Niel, and Mighty Manfred

people who rooted for Cruella de Vil in the movie *101 Dalmations*

"organic" dog food

holistic remedies for canine illnesses

when your dog's diet is more nutritious than yours

when pups are taken away from their mothers too soon, and grow up neurotic

menacing dogs who are really big wimps at heart

when a sleeping dog hogs your spot on the couch

when you have to bring a new baby into "the dog's" home

people who buy lavish presents and gift wrap them for their dogs

when your dog jumps on the bed during an intimate moment

dogs who fetch the newspaper and give it to you torn and soggy with saliva having no idea if the stray who's just nipped you has had her shots

nearly crashing your car to avoid hitting a stray

when Sam has a bad habit of licking his chops until he's given something to eat

when Mocha sneezes all over you

catching a cold from your dog

dognappers

having to get Tippy an identification tattoo

dogs who raise kittens as their own pups

when your dog's neutering operation is
not a howling success and he remains randy

when a dog licks tasty but toxic antifreeze
off the garage floor

when your dog gnaws the head off your
parakeet

dogs who growl when you tickle them

when Candy turns a pillow into a blizzard
of feathers

people with dogs and a wallet full of
pictures of them

listening to someone's long boring story
about a dog they used to own

dogs who grow more and more manic as
you get ready to take them out

when your dog likes to lie in the
high-traffic hallways in your house

giving an eighteen-year-old dog a $30,000
liver transplant

that dogs can be euthanized, but
humans can't

when puppies want to romp at 5:00 A.M.

when your furry Toby jumps on your
clean clothes as soon as you get dressed

bulldogs wearing spiked collars

people who post Marmaduke comics on
the office bulletin board

people who have pictures of their dogs
on their desks

nonowners who can't identify with any of
this nonsense

when your old dog starts having trouble
going up and down stairs

when your dog's whiskers turn gray and
eyes grow cloudy

when old dogs become unhousebroken

when someone calls your incontinent dog
"Winnie the Poop"

when a dog goes to that giant fire hydrant
in the sky

discovering belatedly how attached you
have become to a creature

that a dog's life is nasty, brutish, and short

people who leave their TV on for their
dogs to watch when they're not home

dogs wearing bangs who resemble Moe of
the Three Stooges

when your ankles get flagellated by your dachshund's thrashing tail

trying to calculate how old Roofus is in "dog years"

a dog whose name *should* be "Didshebiteyou?"

when a deceased dog was nasty, brutish, and short—but you miss him anyway

that dogs don't have nine lives

dogs who leave paw prints on your heart